101 USES

FOR a useless ⋏ BANKER

101 USES FOR a useless BANKER

Alex Steuart Williams
with **Sarah Crowther** and **Nick Reid**

JR BOOKS

First published in Great Britain in 2009 by
JR Books, 10 Greenland Street, London NW1 0ND
www.jrbooks.com

A catalogue record for this book is available from the British Library.

ISBN 978-1-906779-63-4

1 3 5 7 9 10 8 6 4 2

Printed and bound by the MPG Books Group

Acknowledgements

This book would never have seen the light of day without the brilliant contributions of Sarah Crowther and Nick Reid, both of whom were steadfast in their dedication to coming up with new ways to torture their former City colleagues. I owe them both a huge debt of gratitude.

Invest in agricultural stocks

Asset stripping

Experiece a real hostile takeover

Receive a performance related bonus

Live in Financial Times

Write Briget Jones's City Diary

Go into teaching

Get a job in government fiscal planning

Become a financial analyst

Personals

Trophy wife, 32 years old, blonde, gorgeous, no sense of humour. Monthly running costs: £7,000.00 pcm. Redundancy forces quick sale. Viewings available at Nobu, Berkeley Square.

Raise money for charity

Cross shareholder investments

Fiscal drag

Become Sir Fred's chief PR spokesman

Help administer the government's
asset protection scheme

Participate in dress-down Fridays

Small business start-up

Shareholder capital calls

Start a pyramid investment scheme

Manage a shrinking endowment

Become a technical investor

Work the trading floor

Short the market

Start a tracker fund

Real estate investing

Reverse takeover

Sales analyst

Invest in seed capital

Issue a promissory note

Establish a senior credit facility

Safety first investing

Invest in samurai bonds

Self-service banking

Re-learn the meaning of the word 'share'

Private banking

Join the public sector

Run out of call options

Commodities trader

Work for a credit rating agency

Advise the government on how to solve the credit crisis

Experience compound interest

Relationship banking

Experience a real banker's draft

Become a lawyer

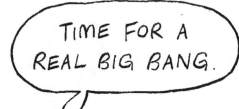

Banking regulation

Become an MP

Run with the bull market

Gilt trading

Floating capital

Diversify into futures and options

Fiscal expansion

Fortune teller

Get into double-barrelled bonds

Electronic wire transfers

Execution-only transactions

Escalator clause contracts

Fiddling expenses

Dead cat bounce

Day trader

Dollar cost averaging

Go long on shorts

Set up a limited partnership

Money laundering

Offshore banking

Stand for parliament

Income stream diversification

Insider dealing

Joint ventures

Independent financial advisor

Diversify into junk bonds

Manage a hedge fund

Start a ponzi scheme

Invest in high risk, high yield bonds

Be a real high-flyer

Government minister

Guilt-edged investments

Human rights activism

When life gives you Lehmans, make Lehmanade

Learn that investments can go down as well as up

Diversify into government securities

Paper recycling

Loss adjustor

Maintain liquidity

Take a real poison pill

Join a city livery company

Asset securitisation

Become a non-dom

Think inside the box

Help the government manage its system
of tripartate regulation

Learn to deal with falling interest rates

Hung, overdrawn and quartered

Alex Steuart Williams is a cartoonist and feature film animator, who knows almost nothing about banking, apart from what he read in the newspaper last week and the garbled bits of half digested information vaguely absorbed over years of dinner party conversation. However, some of his best friends are bankers and he would like to apologise in advance for all the inaccuracies, half-truths, slanders and plain falsehoods within these pages. Not too much though – they do deserve most of it.

Alex also does the Queen's Counsel cartoon strip published weekly in the law pages of *The Times*. Original drawings and prints of his cartoons can be purchased at absurdly reasonable prices at www.qccartoon.com

Previous books by Alex Steuart Williams:

Queen's Counsel – A Libellous Look at the Law
Queen's Counsel 2 – Judgment Day
Queen's Counsel – Laying Down the Law
The Best of Queen's Counsel
*Lawyers Uncovered – Everything You Always Wanted to
    Know But Didn't Want to Pay £500 an Hour to Find Out*
101 Ways to Leave the Law